I0301803

My Life Under the Sonshine

Cassandra F. Lanier

ROYSTON
Publishing

BK Royston Publishing
P. O. Box 4321
Jeffersonville, IN 47131
502-802-5385
http://www.bkroystonpublishing.com
bkroystonpublishing@gmail.com

© Copyright – 2020

All Rights Reserved. No part of this book may be reproduced, stored in a retrieval system, or transmitted by any means without the written permission of the author.

Cover Design: Gad of Elite Book Covers

ISBN-13: 978-1-951941-25-3

Printed in the United States of America

Dedication

This book is dedicated in memory of my daughter Yolanda Dijona Logan who departed this life and took flight to be with the Lord on May 12th, 2018.

At the time of her birth on September 22nd, 1996, I called her my life saver and she's still saving my life today. It is my prayer that you will see how God allowed her life to be an inspiration to many.

Be blessed.

Acknowledgements

I can't even begin without thanking God for always looking beyond my faults, supplying my every need, and keeping me from danger seen and unseen. I am thankful for his son Yeshua/ Jesus, for loving me enough to give His life, and for continuing until this day to intercede to the Father on my behalf. I thank him for not giving up on me and for loving me more than I could ever love myself.

I am forever grateful for my daughters, Danielle and Yolanda Logan, grandsons Antonio Sisson Jr and Bless Jims Saint Louis, and God daughters Kennedi Langston and Lashay Hopson Burl, They have been The Wind Beneath My Wings and the reason that I push as hard as I do to be the best person that I can be. It is because of you and your unconditional love that my life took and stays on a positive course. To my Mom, thank you for loving me and for being a strong spiritual influence in my life, for walking in a way that I would be glad to follow and strive to be as strong, loving and real as you. To my Dad, you have shown me what it is to be a hard worker. We haven't always seen things eye to eye, but I thank God that he has blessed us with time and life challenges to open our eyes to understand each other better, and for me to better understand your love for me. It is also because of you that I am the woman that I have become.

    To all of my family, I love you and thank God for you all. I thank God for being a part of a family that's planted on a strong Foundation of faith and believe in God for me to stand upon and grow. A family that encouraged and continues to encourage and plant seeds of love, hope, and faith into my life.

    To my cousins/ brothers and sisters, it's too many of you all to mention, but I thank you for filling in the gap. In memory of those whose Souls have passed on, I know that you are watching over me. I feel you all the time.

I have to say Thank You to those spiritual leaders that have fed my soul over the years. They gave me the ammunition needed to fight against the power that sometimes knocks me down. But thank God, I always come back up swinging. My pastor Dr. Kevin W Cosby, Dr. Walter Malone, Pastor Antonio Payne, Dr. Anthony Middleton, Pastor Carlton Davis, Pastor Michael George, Pastor Richard Reynolds, Dr. Stacy Spencer, Dr. Christopher Chappelle, and Dr. Cheryl Walker. You might ask the question why so many? Each one of these persons have spoken a life-saving word into my life at one time or another, and some still are, and for that I'm grateful.

To all of my extended children and grandchildren that I have been blessed with over the years, by way of my daughters, I love you and thank you for being a part of my life and my daughter's lives. Thank you all for being there.

Last but not least, I have to thank Mrs. Julia Royston for helping me make this more than just a thought, but a reality.

Table of Contents

Dedication	iii
Acknowledgements	v
Introduction	xi
Meet My Daughter	1
The Accidents	23
The Journey Begins	51
The Journey Continued	61
Peace Through Analogies	113
Life Beyond Tragedy	125
The Race of Life	141

Introduction

July 21st, 1990 would be one of the turning points of my life. That was the day my daughter Danielle was born, and that was the day I really felt God trying to get my attention. Just being honest, I was a little off course, but having her would make me change my way of doing things because it was no longer just me. Things would be okay at first; but eventually, I lost focus again and started treading into even deeper waters.

Although my family was very close on both sides, I still felt like I was missing out on something. I was searching for something. I eventually slipped back into a lifestyle that made me feel accepted and comfortable. I met new friends which brought on new experiences. I thank God that my family on both sides were well rooted and grounded on a firm foundation that was strong and had a relationship with God and His son. If a seed had not been planted, I don't think that I would have had the spirit of discernment to recognize when God had brought me to what I would describe as a crossroad. I believe that he was getting tired of my behavior because he had other plans and things for me to do. Even in the midst of my dirt, he kept interceding to the Father on my behalf.

I believe that in the midst of my dirt, he searched my heart and saw my desire to want better for me and my daughter, but for reasons that I wouldn't even understand until later. It was a struggle to break free, He brought me to yet another crossroad. While still taking my chances and testing my waters, I would get pregnant again. Though my kids have the same father, it was somewhat of a good thing for me but not so good for him because this time he was married. I was faced with abortion, but that wasn't an option for me. Let me say that we all make mistakes, but in this case, what the devil meant for bad, God worked it out for my good.

How could that be good for me? Like I said before, new friends brought on new experiences. Though I never really smoked weed a lot, as time went on, I began to smoke more and later on down the line began to lace my weed. I was living a life that I know wasn't in God's plans for me and things could have gone another way. Although I was mostly a weekend smoker, I never allowed Danielle to see me. I never left any indications that such activities were going on. One particular weekend, Danielle wasn't home, so me and my friend decided to lace the weed. I got so high that I scared myself. My heart was racing so fast. I went into her room and crawled into her bed, and I promised the Lord if he would just make it stop, I would never do it again. I didn't do that anymore, but I did continue to smoke weed.

January 27th, 1996 was my birthday and it had fallen on a Saturday. Because I had slowed down and wasn't really doing anything, my friends decided that they were going to take me out and get me tore up. I had been sick all day, so it had been suggested that I should take a pregnancy test. I quickly said I didn't need one because at that time I wasn't supposed to be seeing anyone. Well, needless to say, I took the test and I was pregnant. Right then and there, I told them to go on without me. I began to feel conviction after conviction, I stopped drinking and smoking at that very moment. Some of my old friends started to fall off, as I had found a new source of strength to distance myself from the things that I had been doing. September 22nd, 1996 will be another life-changing moment for me, Yolanda was born. It was life changing because I had allowed myself to fall into a dark place. Conceiving and giving birth to her brought light into the midst of that darkness that Danielle wasn't old enough to understand that I had fallen in, and I thank God that he protected her from that.

Once released from the hospital, Yolanda was home from the hospital a week and would then have a seizure that gave me the second biggest scare of my life. Mom and Danielle had gone to church, and my father wasn't at home, so it was just me and Yolanda. While she was asleep, I had gone into the kitchen to fix me something to eat. Something told me to go check on her. I guess you could call it Mother's intuition. I picked her up off the bed, and she was stiff and wouldn't respond. Rocking her in my arms, I went to the front door. Just as I began to panic, a friend of mine that has seizures was at the door coming to see her. That was nothing but God. I told her what was happening. She looked at Yolanda and said that she was having a seizure. She said we weren't going to wait on an ambulance, so she drove me to the hospital. I didn't grab anything. I closed the door and we took off. From the time we left the house until we reach the hospital, my baby laid stiff in my arms. When we got there and went inside, they immediately took her and put an oxygen mask on her and she began to cry. Right then and there I vowed to stay on course and be the best mother I could be for my daughters. I had made up my mind that a life that wasn't good enough for them, wasn't good enough for me. That's why I call Yolanda my lifesaver. They both made life-saving changes for the good in my life because they were both conceived at times in my life that God was trying to get my attention. It's just the conviction was stronger, and I was no longer willing to take the chance.

Now don't get me wrong, my friends were not bad people. We just were not doing the same things anymore. I can still call them friends today, because they understood what I was trying to do, and they never tried to get me to waiver in any way. Those are true friends. God began to place people in my life that made it easier to stay on course. He placed people in my life that had a different outlook on life. Felicia Smith would be one of them, and because of her I was blessed with my goddaughter Kennedi. Of course, the powers that be, never stopped trying with his sneaky tactics, but God's way prevailed.

In around 2005, God put it on my heart to start a family newsletter. I called it the 'Family Connection' because I felt like we were losing the family closeness that I had grown up around. There was also a thought planted in my mind to write a book. I even had a title, 'My Life Under The Sonshine.' There were particular talk shows at that time going around different states sharing the hardships of people's lives. After hearing some of those stories, I thought to myself, 'God ain't told you to write a book.' So, the thought quickly left my mind, but I did start working on my newsletter. Over the years, I eventually stop writing those because it just seemed that nobody was getting what I was trying to do. I always felt like God had something for us to do as a family, but little by little for whatever reason, it just seemed like the family was slowly drifting farther apart.

Fast forward to 2018, God's truly been good. I haven't been perfect, and I've made my share of mistakes, but Thanks be to God, I never looked back. I've continued to press forward and grow learning more and more each day. As you can see that book that was just a thought years ago is now a reality. Maybe God knew something that I didn't even see coming. It's been a journey, but my daughters, grandsons' parents and just my overall love for my family, has given me the strength to keep it moving, whatever might come my way. So, in all reality, they are all my life savers. Well, something hit my life before 2018 could come and go that I could have never imagined. Five people that I love dearly would go home to be with the Lord. Among those five would be my youngest daughter. Not only did she save my life in 1996, she is still saving it until this very day and is the inspiration for me writing this book.

It is my prayer as I share my experiences as I go through my process of grief, I hope that it will help someone and that they might be able to see God.

Yolanda and Cassandra

Bless and Antonio

Cassandra and Danielle

My Life Under the Sonshine

Meet My Daughter

Yolanda Dijona Logan, born September 22nd, 1996. As I stated before, Yolanda was born at a time that I was at yet another crossroad in my life. She gave me that extra strength to fight harder to do better for her and her sister. She was full of life so energetic, lovable, smart, feisty, and her smile with those dimples was magnetic. She just had this magnetic personality from a baby into her young adult life. It was us against the world. We were the 'Three Musketeers.'

As Yolanda got older, she began to show signs of wanting more. I think she felt like a complete family consists of a father, mother, and the kids. So, with that being said, I guess in her eyes we were never complete. I would notice how she would look at fathers when they would be with their kids and the comments she would make. I could feel that she wanted that as well; although, my life was on a better path it was still complicated. She would want me to talk to anybody. She didn't care who it was, and all he would have to do is say, "Hi." She would say, "Get him mama, he wants you." I was kind of afraid to bring anyone around, because if I did, she would want to know if they were going to be her stepdad. So along with the personal fears of being hurt and the fear of having two girls and her eagerness to want a man around, I made a decision to just be alone. I raised my girls the best way I could because in my mind they had a father. At that time, I felt like I had made the right decision, but I would later be faced with the fact that that may have been the worst thing I could have done.

Yolanda was a child that just made you smile and shake your head, even in her early age. She was very smart and a very good reader at a young age. I can't remember exactly how old she was, but it was one Christmas. My Uncle Greg was so impressed with how good she read that he asked her if she wanted to read the Christmas story from the Bible, and she did. She loved the attention and that was the difference between her and Danielle. Danielle was quiet and laid-back, and Yolanda was my loud, look at me child. They were night and day and being 6 years apart that kind of caught me off guard. Quiet and laid-back was the norm for me, because that's how I was.

Life wasn't bad, we would move from our little two-bedroom apartment out on 7th Street, to a two-bedroom townhouse off of 16th and Chestnut. Just wanting more room and what I felt was better for us. In 2001, we would move into our dream home that would later turn out to be more of a nightmare. Danielle would later tell me they were satisfied being in the townhouse and things were better then. I didn't understand it then, but I would later understand that we were closer. Once we moved to our new home, things were still good, but it was more responsibility, more space and room for mistakes. It was a tri-level house on the corner, 3 bedrooms, a nice-sized kitchen, living room, a family room, playroom, washroom and a garage. The backyard was already equipped with a swing set with the big slide. It was perfect and nothing short of a blessing. Yolanda had her own room and she wanted it decorated with the Powder Puff Girls. It was fitting because she had that kind of energy. She always had someone staying over, but I didn't mind. I would rather have her at home. She was only allowed to stay at 2 friends' houses, and they were both right across the street unless it was family. She could never sit still. She always had to be doing something or going somewhere which kept me and her sister going.

At the age of 10, Yolanda's mannerism and attitude begin to change. She started acting out at school and at home. I was not really understanding how she could go from being this happy-go-lucky child, to being a child that was always cutting up and acting out. That just wasn't her and I didn't know what to do. I took her to the doctor, and she was diagnosed with ADHD. She's put on medication, but she was still acting out. All the medication was doing was just making her depressed, and she would just break out crying for no reason. I couldn't take what that medicine was doing to her, so we tried some type of patch. It slowed her down, but she was still acting out. Not knowing what else to do, I just stopped going to that doctor because it just seemed like all they wanted to do was keep trying different medications and have her doped up. I found another doctor's office, and this doctor would be a little different. Although she also prescribes the same medications for ADHD, she also didn't like the effect that it had on kids and she wanted to try other options before starting that medication. I was good with that, so we changed her diet. Things got a little better, but she was still doing things that just didn't make sense.

Time went on and she continued to act out in school and at home. Just not knowing how to handle it, I began to shut down. Not realizing it, I began to place a lot of responsibilities on her sister that she didn't need. I was working third shift, and I thought at that time that would be best because they would be asleep while I was at work. Those hours seem to work best for me, but I eventually found out that for many reasons that wasn't a good idea at all.

Fast forwarding to her freshman year of high school. She had gotten suspended and one of the requirements of the suspension was to get counseling. The lady that I spoke with gave me a list with counselor's names, if I didn't have one in mind. This one particular name stood out to me, Shannon Hines. She told me that I made a good choice because she was one of the best ones on the list. To this very day, I believe God had his hands in that decision. She was so humble, Spirit-filled, and Yolanda just took to her like they had always known one another. After a couple of visits, I realized that she wasn't just counseling Yolanda, but she was counseling me as well. After telling Shannon Yolanda's behavior and the problems I was having, she asked me if Yolanda had been molested. I told her not that I knew of, but I always asked her if anybody had ever messed with her. She would always say, "No." That was something that I just always asked them. She went on to tell me that from what I said, and her talking to Yolanda, she felt something had happened. Maybe it was someone that she knew and she didn't want to get them in trouble. About a year or so into counseling, Yolanda finally broke down one day. While doing my usual fussing and making comparisons telling her what she could and should be doing, she finally just yelled out, "You don't know what I've been through and you don't know me." When I asked her to talk to me and to help me understand, she wouldn't talk to me. She only wanted to talk to Shannon. I called Shannon and let her know what happened. She scheduled an appointment for Yolanda to come to her office. On the day of the session, her and Yolanda talked first, and then she called me into the office. She informed me that Yolanda had given her permission to tell me what they had discussed. Shannon began to tell me what they talked about. My worst fear had happened. She had been molested by a boy in the neighborhood. She said that it had only happened once, but this young man would continue to come around the house and she never said a word. She went on to say that he was going with one of her friends and tried to mess with little girls in the neighborhood. When I asked her if he had ever tried anything with her, she told me, "No." I just remember feeling numb and fighting back my tears. When I asked her why she didn't say anything when she was asked, she would say something that hurt me to the core of my heart. She told me that she didn't say anything because I didn't listen to her when she told me that they didn't need to be home by themselves. She still wasn't telling me nothing. At that point, all I could say was I'm sorry and that I never meant for anything like that to ever happen to her. My apology was accepted. A big load was lifted off of her that day. For over 6 years, she had built a wall and created this person within herself that protected her from all hurt and harm. It really was destroying her and causing her to make bad choices, but she couldn't see it at first. There is one thing my daughter Danielle taught me. She would always say, "To thine own self be true." The truth of the matter was, although I was trying to raise them to be God-fearing, independent, respectful young ladies, I was naive in thinking that I was doing the right things. I had failed them in so many ways. I thank God they loved me beyond my mistakes and knew that I loved them with all my heart. Everything I did was for them.

Just looking back over the years after she had that breakthrough, things began to make sense. Can you imagine being 10 years old and dealing with that by yourself because you feel like everyone that said they loved you allowed that to happen? Those same people are expecting so much of you. They don't even seem to try to understand you. They're always fussing and complaining that you can't do anything right. Eventually you start feeling that way about yourself. Mind you, nobody knew what had happened or what she was going through all of that time, but unknowingly, we added to the load that she was already carrying. She dealt with it the best way that she could. The devil had his plan, but God had his plans as well. When she was getting in trouble in school, it was about to drive me nuts. Now I can say that I'm glad that she got suspended. It led us to a woman that had the love of God in her heart, and she saw something in Yolanda that would move her to just want to be a part of her life. Yolanda loved going to counseling. They would both light up when they saw each other. Yolanda also had a phobia about going because she felt like having to go to counseling made her crazy. It was finally agreed upon that making Yolanda come to counseling wouldn't be productive. When she didn't want to be there she wouldn't participate. Shannon told her to just call her whenever she needed to come in and she would make sure to get her into the office. She kept her word to Yolanda. Every time Yolanda called, Shannon got her in as soon as possible and she was there every time. I can look back on it now and smile because Yolanda wouldn't always be by herself. A lot of times, she would take her boyfriend at the time, a friend, one of her cousins, and Shannon never said a word. I think Yolanda was trying to get everybody counseling. She would tell them that they needed help too. I thank God that we crossed paths with someone that had a genuine concern for Yolanda, what was going on in her life and the people she was surrounding herself with.

I can honestly say that Yolanda feeling comfortable enough to include me in on most of her sessions, helped us a lot. We began to get closer and be able to talk about what or how she was feeling about things that affected her or things that bothered me. We still bumped heads but at least now, we were trying to find ways to fix things. It would still be a struggle. Although she had lost the weight of the burden she had been carrying, she was now in a constant fight with the person she had created that didn't feel or wouldn't allow anyone to hurt her. It would still be a hard thing to deal with and even harder thing to watch. She would tell me and my mom, "I'm trying to do better, but it's like something just overpowers me." There were times you could look in her eyes and see that loving person you knew that was trapped inside of this person that wouldn't let her out. She continued to get knocked down by some bad choices and not being able to find where she fit into society. For almost six years, she was just going through the motions of life and now she's about to be a young adult and time has passed her by. She would get knocked down, but she never stayed down for long. She always kept fighting. That is one of the things I've always been proud of both of my daughters for and that is never giving up no matter what. That always encouraged me. To this day, I haven't experienced some of the things that they have in their lifetime. It's a different era of time and things are much more different and complicated. I would always let her know when she helped me out. Once Yolanda opened up, she never had a problem speaking her mind. It didn't always come out nice, but you got it. I just believe that you're never too old to learn and sometimes those lessons might come by way of your kids.

From an early age until Yolanda's passing, she always had to have people around. I would always tell her to stop acting needy and asked why she couldn't be by herself. She would say, "You got me messed up. I'm not needy." It wouldn't be until my baby passed that I would get to know her even more. I messed up and missed out on some awesome things while she was here because I was focusing on the negative energy that surrounded her. She always said that she didn't like people but had the biggest heart and was always trying to help someone in any way that she could. Even to the extent of getting herself involved in other people's battles. Don't get me wrong. She could be mean and say things to hurt your feelings. I must say that I did feel sorry for her friends sometimes. She would talk to them so bad. They might take a break, but they would be right back. Me and mom would just laugh and shake our heads because it just seemed like they were asking for punishment. We didn't understand it then, but we got it later. She met them where they were, and what seemed harsh to us, they understood it.

Yolanda never met a stranger. She had 3 best friends that she didn't play about. Shavon passed away in May of 2017, and then there was Savannah and Julius. Everyone else was either her mom, dad, aunt, uncle, sister, brother, and everybody was her friend. Of course, we had something negative to say about her knowing so many people. I had so many people young and old to come up to me and tell me the impact she made on their lives, but it was obvious from the love shown at the service. I thank God for the opportunity to get to understand and know her better. I miss her like crazy, but we have a new relationship now. It's not physical but spiritual. She is still my sidekick, and we're still a team. There are some things I'm still learning because of her. We had this saying between me, mom and my girls that we would always tell one another, 'That We're In It Together,' and we still are. Though she's absent from the body, her presence is still felt so strong. I get it now. There was something about just being in her presence. I guess to sum Yolanda up. She was a young, free spirited, and not perfect by any means, just living the life of most people her age. She was goofy and brought life to any dull situation. She could be loving and mean all at the same time. You couldn't even stay mad at her for long before she'd have you shaking your head and laughing. One thing I know that she would want me to say, because she always said it to me in our talks, "When I love someone, I love hard and I just want that love in return."

I would like to share a story as I close this chapter. Yolanda's friend that went to middle school with her stopped by the house one day to check on me. As we were talking, she went on to tell me that her and Yolanda had fallen out over something silly. She went on to say that they really hadn't been close for a long time and only spoke when they would see each other. It wasn't because Yolanda didn't try, but it was her fault for being stubborn. She told me that she had to show up at the hospital to let Yolanda know that she was there, and she was sorry and that she loved her. She then went on to tell me how Yolanda had been there for her during

Middle School and felt like Yolanda had saved her life. She reminded me of times she would be at my house when I got off from work, and I wouldn't know she was there until they started bumping around. She had been running away from home and going to the park, and Yolanda had told her to just come to our house so that she wouldn't have to worry about her. Of course, she said it in her way. Then she went on to tell me about another time that Yolanda spoke something into her life, and it made her want to turn her life around. Yolanda was making an impact way back then. At the end of the conversation, she said something that really stuck with me. "Momma Cass, do you know how they say be careful because you never know when you are entertaining an angel? What if she was an angel?" So, with that being said, you have just met my daughter, my BAP#2, a part of what made me who I have become, my Angel.

A Very Happy Day for Yolanda headed to Prom.

Yolanda and her sister with their godmother, "Yolanda" her namesake.

The Accidents

Danielle, her boyfriend and the boys had just been home for Easter, but she had decided to come back home for Derby weekend which is the first weekend in May. We were all looking forward to them coming back soon. May would bring about another life-changing experience for me. I was working second shift, but I received a job bid to start first shift May 13th. I had switched shifts because my grandson wanted to come for the summer, and I figured it would give me more time to see Yolanda. We were starting to plan trips for the summer something that was long overdue.

Being that I had just lost my friend in January and then turned around in February and lost my aunt, I had made up my mind that I was going to sit them down and tell them where the policies were and discuss what I wanted done if anything were to happen to me. Well, it's the week of Derby, and Yolanda had stopped by the house. I went on to tell her my plans to talk to them when her sister got home. I told her that I wanted to be cremated. She looked at me and smacked her lips and said, "Don't burn me up. Put me in the ground, and I want a blue casket. I want to be in blue." Then she named some rap song she wanted played. I told her, "Girl, I'm not playing no rap song." We both laughed and then she said, "I don't want no singing, play music." I was like, "Okay girl," and we both laughed again.

It's May 4th, and I'm about to head to work, but I called Danielle to see if they had left Georgia. They were already on the road, and she said that they should be arriving around 3 o'clock. I headed on to work and called again once I got my first break. I knew that they should have been close or already in town, but when I called, I didn't get an answer. I kept trying until the end of my break, still no answer. I worked for a little bit and went to my locker to check my phone to see if she had called me back, nothing. I continued to work, but I couldn't focus and then I got this sick feeling in my stomach. I went to my team leader and told her that I had to leave because I couldn't focus and that I wasn't feeling right because I hadn't heard from my daughter. I clocked out and right when I opened the door to my car my phone wrung. I knew that it was her, but before I could say anything I heard the trembling in her voice and she said, "Mama, we've been in an accident. Can you please come?"

I told her, "Believe it or not, I'm getting in my car as we speak because I couldn't work because I hadn't heard from you." She told me where they were located. I made it from Port Road in Jeffersonville Indiana to the Gene Snyder exit on 65 in Louisville in about 20 minutes and thank goodness I didn't get a ticket. She told me that she thought everyone was okay, and they were all being checked out in the ambulance. When I pulled up and saw the car, my heart dropped. All I could do was say, "Thank you Jesus, Thank you God."

It was raining and the car had hydroplaned, hit the median and landed back out into the highway. A car hit them and knocked them off the highway into a grassy area that was filled with muddy water. I walked up to the ambulance and someone opened the door, and she was the first one I saw. I could tell that she was shook up and she was shaking. Then, I saw her boyfriend and the boys. My grandson Bless was 8 months at the time. He was fine. He only had a scratch on his chest from the car seat. My grandson Antonio had a knot on his head and a big knot on the side of his knee. Her boyfriend was complaining of chest pain. It was a relief to see that no one was seriously hurt. No one wanted to ride in the ambulance, so I drove them to the hospital myself so that they could be evaluated. Before leaving the site of the accident, her and myself got in that dirty water and got what we could out of the car because it wasn't going to be able to be towed until the next day.

On the way to the hospital, she told me what happened. They had stopped one last time for gas around Bowling Green. She said, coming out of the store she had looked up into the sky, and then she told them to look because she felt like something was looking at her. They got the gas. For some reason, before they took off, Antonio switched the baby's car seat to the other side, and they proceeded on to Louisville. They had made it into Louisville and that's when the car hydroplaned. One car swerved and missed them, but the second car hit right smack in the middle of the passenger side knocking them off the highway. She said all that she could think to do was jump out of the car and check on the boys in the backseat. She saw that Tonio was okay, and she snatched the baby out of the car seat. She said that he was laughing. She said, "Mama, Antonio had been laying down on the seat and he had just set up. Antonio told me that his first instinct was to grab his brother's car seat, because he saw it tilting. I told him that I was proud of him and that he was his brother's keeper. After she told me everything, I told her that someone was watching over them for Antonio to change the seating arrangement before they got back on the road. The impact from the car pushed the front seat into the back seat where the baby's seat would have been and where Tonio had been laying. For them to only come out with bumps and bruises, the baby being perfectly fine and laughing, and to think that could have been a semi-truck that hit them, yes someone was watching over them.

    Me and my father got up the next morning and went to meet the tow truck driver. When he saw the car, all he could do was shake his head and say, "Uh, uh, uh." I knew what he meant because in all reality that could have been worse than it was. They were sore the next day, but that was to be expected. Needless to say, the conversation I had planned to have never took place and that was the furthest thing on my mind. All I could do was think about how I could have lost my family in that car accident. They were leaving on Sunday, so of course, a car had to be rented to get them back home until they got things situated. Yolanda stopped by the house so that she could see them before they got on the road. We were standing around in the dining room. So, I told both of them to come on and let's get together and take a picture because after what had happened you just never know. They didn't want to take the picture because they said we looked ratchet, but I told them I didn't care. So, we took the picture, and everybody laughed because Yolanda had her famous bonnet on.

May 11th, I was up early because I had an appointment to get my oil changed. Yolanda called me around 8:30 or so, but I didn't answer the phone because I thought I knew what she wanted. She left me a message, so I said I would just call when I got back home. I was going to show her a little tough love. I had to be at work at 12:30, so when I got home, I went on and proceeded to get ready for work. I called, but she didn't answer. Normally, she would have called me right back, but I knew that she didn't have a phone and she was using her boyfriend's phone. It was around 11:15 to 11:30, and I tried again, but still no answer. So, I left her a message because I figured she was only calling because I was supposed to leave her some money. So, I told her where it would be. Something tells me to call her back again but still no answer. I left another message instead. I told her regardless of what anyone may have told her that I loved her very much. I've made some mistakes, but not answering the phone was the biggest mistake of my life, and you're about to find out why.

I headed for work, I had just made it across the bridge and was headed down the road that led to my job. I was just about there and my phone rung. I thought it was Yolanda, but it was Danielle. Her voice was trembling, and I thought something was wrong with her or the boys. That wasn't the case. She went on to tell me that someone kept calling her phone, but she wouldn't answer because she didn't know who it was. They wouldn't stop, so she finally answered. They told her that Yolanda had been in a bad car accident and the ambulance took her to the hospital, but her boyfriend had died at the scene. With nervousness in her voice, she said, "You need to call Yolanda or something and find out what's going on, and please call me back as soon as possible, please. I hung up and called my job. I told them that I wouldn't be there, that my daughter had been in a car accident, and I didn't know what was going on. Not knowing what to think or do, I began to panic. As I was turning around to head back towards Louisville, I called my mom to let her know what happened. She told me to call the police to see if they knew what hospital she had been taken to, but they didn't know. I called my best friend Sheniqua. She told me to go to University hospital because that was where they took trauma situations.

I had made it back across the bridge, and I was only blocks away from the hospital. I got there, parked and hurried into the emergency room sign in desk. I asked her if Yolanda Logan had been brought there. As she's looking it up, the chaplain walks up and introduces herself. I asked her if she was okay, and this woman just turns around and says follow me.

I said it again, "Is she okay?"
She still doesn't say anything.

So, then I was like, "So, she's not okay?"

Finally, she looks at me with this dry look and says, "I'm going to sit you in this room. If you have any more family members coming, I'll take you all up once they get her ready to be seen."

Once again, I ask, "Is she okay?"

She finally says, "It doesn't look good, but the doctor will be able to better explain things to you." My heart just starts to pound. I'm shaking, and I start to beat myself up because I didn't answer the phone when she called. The night before the accident, I had gone to her house because I had reasons to be concerned. When I finally got in to see her, she was asleep. All I needed to see was that she was okay, so I didn't wake her up. She was sleeping so peacefully, and I didn't want to wake her up because I know she had trouble sleeping. I saw her keys sitting on her dresser, so I took them so that her boyfriend couldn't take off in her car. He must have noticed it after I left and woke her up, because she called me upset and wanted her keys back. I wasn't far from the house, so I turned around and took them back. I was going to take them back the next morning because I knew I had to be up early. I knew that she had running around to do. To top it off, I didn't answer the phone when she called.

I called Danielle and told her it was true, but I didn't know anything yet, because they were still working on her. I felt like s*** having to tell her that, because I had called her when I went to her house to check on her. She knew that I had taken her keys back. There I was, her boyfriend's dead, she's in the hospital and I don't know what to expect. Her dad arrived, and then my parents. By this time, the chaplain is ready to take us up to the Intensive Care Unit. She places us in this little room that sets adjacent to the hospital rooms. My cousins Debra and Jeannie arrived. We're all sitting there talking try not to think the worst. Then the head nurse walks in. She begins to introduce herself. To my surprise, it's a member of my church. We once sung in the choir together. She began to tell us that they've never seen anything like it before, she was in pretty bad shape, and that the doctors would be in to explain in more detail shortly. She told us that once they got her cleaned up, that we would be able to go into her room.

Finally, the doctors came in, introduced themselves and told us what they specialize in. One of them began to speak.

He says, "This is something that we hate to do, but things don't look good. We lost her, we were able to bring her back, but she's in a coma."

He went on to say that her skull was twisted, she was brain dead and losing a lot of blood. It was like I went deaf for a minute after he said that and I just saw his lips moving. This couldn't be happening, not again. Danielle's accident was just the week before. I'm thinking, 'Lord, please let her be alright.' Then I heard him say that even if she came out of the coma, she would be a vegetable. At that point, I didn't know what to think. He went on to say that they would continue to give her blood and do all that they could do. They would give it more time and do the test again, but we would eventually have to make a decision. They asked if we had any questions. Like I said, I was numb. I can't remember if anyone said anything.

I do remember us having prayer after the doctors left the room. When her dad was done with the prayer, he looked at me and said, "Well." We both knew that if it came down to it, Yolanda wouldn't want to be a vegetable. She was a free spirit and she couldn't be still. She was always on the go. Her life would never be the same. We made the decision to pull the plug if they came back asking us to make a decision.

Deep down knowing what Yolanda would want but hoping that it wouldn't come to that. They finally came in and told us that we could go see her, but to prepare ourselves. I walked in first, broke down and went right out. That wasn't my baby lying there. She wasn't even recognizable. Her face was so swollen, machines and tubes were running through her everywhere. I think everybody else stayed in her room. I pulled myself together and went back in, but I didn't stay long. I pray that she understood. I just couldn't take seeing her like that. I went back in again, but I stood toward the head of the bed just to the side of her. I could somewhat take seeing her from that position. I looked at the side of her head and her hand, but I couldn't look into her face. I stayed long enough to tell her that I loved her, and that I was sorry for not answering the phone. The devil had started his attack on me. I started to have all types of thoughts, and I rubbed her hand and walked out of the room. By this time, I guess the word was out about the accident, because family and friends began to arrive at the hospital. Yolanda always told me that I needed to toughen up because she felt like I was too nice and soft spoken. To her, that was being weak or like a punk. As I was leaving the room, it was like something came over me. I kept hearing, "Don't be no punk, Danielle and Tonio needs you, they're going to need you." From that moment on, I knew that I had to be strong for my family and her friends, but most of all, for her.

We left the room so that others could go in. I can't remember who called Danielle; me or her dad, but the call was made to let her know what the doctors said. She asked that we please keep her posted. I pray that she forgives me, because I couldn't just sit in the room and look at her like that. I stayed out in the hall, waiting room area, and then I would go back in. I can remember being in the room one time and the coordinator from Kentucky Organ Donor's

Affiliates came into the room. She introduced herself and told us that Yolanda was a registered organ donor. I think she basically wanted to know how we felt about it being that it was a possibility that we would be faced with the decision of pulling the plug. We didn't know that she had done it, but we were in agreement with her all the way. What person in their right mind would not be in agreement with someone who wanted to give the gift of life? Besides, we already knew about organ donor. My mom was a liver transplant recipient and someone did the same act of kindness for her. We were very proud of her decision to do such a selfless act, but that was Yolanda. She asked if she could speak with me and her dad, so we stepped out of the room. She just wanted to let us know that if it came down to us making the decision to pull the plug, another coordinator from KODA would be coming to assist us and that she was very nice. We told her thank you and went back into the room.

In the midst of all that was going on, we were trying to figure out how to reach her friend's parents because he wasn't from Louisville. I thank God for my cousin, because she was able to figure out how to get in touch with his son's mother. She came to the hospital, and I'm not sure but I think that she got in touch with his family. People were still coming to the hospital. We were all over the place, in her room, outside of the room, in the hallway and the waiting room. The hospital staff never said a word. We weren't loud or disrespectful to the other patients. We were just praying and waiting. I remember going back into the room just standing there. I looked at the back of her head. I could see a Bantu knot sticking out from under the bandage that she had wrapped around her head. I could see how straight it was. I had been fussing at her to get something done to her head. She told me if I didn't like it, to get it done. So, I bought the stuff she needed so that my cousin Cardonya could do her hair. She was in town, because her father had passed. I just smiled and told her that I could see that she had gotten her hair done. I know that it looked pretty. I felt myself about to get emotional, so I walked out of the room. One of her friends had given me a phone charger, so I went into the waiting room to charge my phone. I had been standing there for a few minutes and suddenly became overwhelmed. I went into the bathroom and just broke down. I fell to my knees and told the Lord, "I didn't know what to do." I asked him to give me strength to deal with whatever his will was, because I wasn't going to be able to make it without him. I asked him to please forgive me, if I had failed Yolanda in anyway. I heard a knock on the door, and I believe it was my cousin Debra asking me if I was alright.

I told her, "Yes." I got myself together and walked out. They told me that her dad was looking for me. I found him and we went into the little room across from her.

"Well," he says. "They need for us to make a decision."

We're just sitting there looking at each other in disbelief that it had come down to what we had hoped it wouldn't. The decision had already been made earlier. It was just a matter of telling the doctors.

We had to do something that was about to be even harder. We had to call Danielle and let her know what we were about to do. She was already about to get on the road, but she asked us not to do anything until she got to the hospital. I'm so glad that she still had the rental car. After we told Danielle, we told everyone at the hospital. That was hard as well, because some of her friends were there. They were crying and asking us not to do it. It kind of made me second guess myself, because they would cry out that Yolanda was a fighter. She was a fighter, but God had put in my spirit that she was ok. She didn't have to fight anything anymore.

He told me not to look at, or get caught up into the tragedy, but to see the blessing. At that moment, I saw beyond the flesh that housed her soul. I believe that Yolanda had already taken flight and she was safe. I just kept telling myself that God didn't make mistakes. I still had so much to be thankful for. I could have lost my whole family within a week's time. What lay there was what I knew of her. We started a new relationship which was a spiritual connection. I was able to go into the room and tell her that I loved her. She didn't have to worry about being misunderstood, hurt, mistreated, always being fussed at, criticized, no more restless nights, no more worries, and no more heartache.

    I called her best friend in California to let her know. She hadn't been long given birth to her son, Ramier. Yolanda was his Godmother.

    She said the same thing her other friends said, "Mom, are you sure? Can't you just wait? Yolanda's a fighter." I felt bad, because she wanted to come but she wasn't going to be able to make it. I told her that Yolanda would understand. I am so grateful for our family and friends that were able to make it to the hospital to show their love and support. Just about everybody stayed at the hospital even after we made our decision. My uncle Gregory and Aunt Sandra had drove from Huntsville, AL. He had prayer a few times while he was at the hospital. He kept saying, "Yolanda's spirit is strong." I couldn't have agreed with him more, even though it was a time of pain and sorrow. It was as if you could feel her presence. There was a sense of peace and calmness. Even though satan tried to take me to a dark place many times, I refused to give him anything, all Glory was going to God. I know without a shadow of doubt, that if God wanted to work things out another way, He could have. Prayers continued to be lifted for strength and for traveling grace for Danielle, Haiti and the boys. Praises continued to be lifted to God, because even in the midst of the tragedy, God was still good. This was just the beginning of me seeing God moving in a mighty way.

After we made our decision, the other coordinator from KODA had made it to the hospital. I didn't meet her right away. Yolanda's dad, my Uncle Greg and Aunt Sandra had already met and spoke with her. I believe that I was on my way back into the room, and William stopped me so that I could meet her.

She went on to introduce herself, "I'm Kim Whitlow. First, let me say that I'm sorry for your loss. What Yolanda has done is a very selfless act. I know you must be proud of her. If you need anything, I am here for you and your family to try and make this moment go as smooth as possible. If you need anything, I mean it, you let me know."

Then she went on to describe herself which made me smile. She went on to explain the process and what would take place, but she did it in a way that brought you comfort at a very sad time. It was something unique about her spirit. She really just blended in like she was a part of the family.

I was somewhat on an emotional roller coaster the whole time. We were now just waiting for Danielle to make it to the hospital. By the time Danielle made it in town, I was in a better place and praying that I would be able to be strong enough for her and Antonio. Me and her dad went down to meet them. Of course, the devil tried once again to attack me. When they walked into the hospital, I told them that I was glad that they had made it safely, I hugged Antonio and the baby, and I was trying to say something to her but she just walked right past me and went to her dad. We began to walk to the elevators.

I told her dad, "She's mad at me. She walked right past me." I started to cry. I went back to beating myself up.

"It's all my fault, I shouldn't have taken her those keys back." That's how the devil works, but he didn't win again because she turned around and gave me a hug. I told her that I thought that she was mad at me.

She said, "Mama, No. You just have to understand. I'm all the way in Georgia and I got the call." For a moment, I hadn't thought that even though she knew what was going on, she was just as numb as I was. They were really close. Everybody that had stayed at the hospital was waiting for Danielle when we got off the elevator. They all began to hug her and tell her that they loved her. After she was done hugging everyone, I asked her if she was ready to go into the room. She was kind of shaking a little bit, but she took a deep breath and said, "Yes." As we were walking towards the room, I tried to prepare her just as the nurse tried to prepare us. She entered the room and just broke down crying, "They called me Yolanda. They called me first and I came. They knew to call me first and I came."

I thank God for the strength to be able to fight back my tears and comfort her. Like I said, I had never been to the other side of the bed, but I looked at my grandson as he watched his mother crying. I don't think it had hit him yet. As I looked at her, I almost wanted to break down all over again. I stood next to Antonio and I put my arms around him.

He looked up at me and said, "Na Nu, she's going to get better."

I told him, "No, things were pretty bad."

He started to cry and said, "That's not fair. I was supposed to buy her a house."

I told him, "But, you can still buy her a house. Do everything you told her you would do. Buy that house and put her picture in a room. You can still make her proud of you, okay?"

He said, Okay!" We were informed that they wouldn't be doing anything until Sunday, so we stayed a little bit longer. It was really late and there was nothing else we could do. We knew that she was okay because the nurses have been taking great care of her the whole time we were there. Kim was there, like I said, she had stepped in just like a part of the family. We left to get rested up for the next day. As we got off the elevators heading to our cars, I was still numb and somewhat in disbelief of what had just taken place. I watched her dad and his wife as they walked down the hallway towards the parking garage. I couldn't even begin to imagine what they may have been feeling. I knew that his wife loved her as well. I looked at Danielle. Yes, I had just lost my baby girl, but they had lost far more. He just buried his mom in October of 2012, his son passed on June 23rd of 2017 right around his mother's birthday and it was coming up on a year of his passing and not even a year after the passing of his first born, William who was 32. He would have to suffer yet another loss, our baby. She would have been 22 in 4 months. Danielle has suffered that same loss, and I know it was an even heavier burden for her.

The Journey Begins

It's Saturday morning, and I opened my eyes wishing that it was all a dream, but it was not. My baby was really gone. It's just all so surreal. I laid there for a minute because I can't seem to make myself get up. I look up towards the ceiling and start crying. As I'm making myself get up, I thank the Lord for another day and then I said, "Good morning, Yodie, I love you. Lord, thank you for another day. Please give me strength to get through this day. All right, Yodie let's get this day started. In eight more days, it will be a year and 4 months since Yolanda's passing, and that's how I started my day every day.

My mom and dad are early risers, so they were already up. Mom was in the bathroom putting on her makeup. We both tell each other good morning, and then she asked me how I was. I told her that I was okay, but I just couldn't believe that just a week ago I could have lost Danielle and the kids. Turn around a week later and it's the same thing and I lose Yolanda. No disrespect, but I felt like I was in some Whitney Houston and Bobbi Kristina type stuff. I didn't understand how I was feeling. I was rejoicing, I was sad and heartbroken all at the same time. I was telling her and still telling myself that God makes no mistakes, but why now. We had always been talking about we needed to take a real family trip. Not just going to Georgia to see Danielle and the kids, but all of us coming together and going out of town somewhere together and we were finally doing that. We were planning a trip to Florida for the summer. Her and I had already planned to go to Alabama, why now? She always said I worked too much and was always too tired to do anything, I had just put in a job bid to start working first shift on the 13th of May so that we could hopefully spend more time together. Why now, when it seemed like everything was falling into place?

We just began to start sharing stories with one another, talking and laughing. Mom began to cry.

She said, "Yolanda would have me so upset sometimes. She would just get me out of my character, she chuckled and wiped her tears. "But I know that wasn't the Yolanda I knew and loved. I'm crying, but I know that she is with God, and we don't know what he saw coming ahead of her. I just believe in my heart, that he said before I let that happen, I'll give her rest from all of her pain."

We were both in agreement on that. I love my mom for her strength and faith in God. Little does she know how much she has helped me just watching her walk with the Lord. While talking with her, I shared a moment with her that I had while standing beside Yolanda, because I didn't think anyone else would understand. I went on to tell her that, as I was standing next to Yolanda looking at her swollen face and the blood that was on it, I thought about Jesus. Now, before I go any further, I don't want anyone to think that I'm calling her Jesus or even putting her on the same level. I thought of Jesus because of the atmosphere that was present at the hospital. I thought about Jesus because God had told me not to get caught up in the tragedy but to see the blessings. I thought of Jesus because of the blood that was still on her face even after they had cleaned her up as much as they could. I thought of Jesus because I felt a shift in the atmosphere, I didn't know if anyone else felt it. I told my mom that they always say, take up your cross and follow him. I believe that she did just that. She laid down sacrificing her happiness trying to make others happy. She laid down the heartache, pain and criticism, but yet, I had a feeling that her work down here wasn't done. I told her that scriptures and sayings that I had heard were coming to me with new meaning. I felt like I was crazy or something, but my mom told me that I wasn't because she had felt the same thing watching the nurse coming in and of the room changing the towels that were soaked with her blood. I told her that I couldn't remember the nurse coming in and out of the room, because I only focused on one place or else I wouldn't have been able to stay in the room as long as I did. She told me that I wasn't crazy, and that I hadn't seen anything yet. She was right.

After I finished talking with my mom, I went upstairs to check on Danielle to see if she was awake and to see if she wanted to go to the hospital. She got up and started to get ready. I got what I needed from upstairs and went back downstairs. I walked into the kitchen and looked out of the window and saw my father in the backyard, I can see the pain all over his face. Tears began to fill my eyes and I told Yolanda, "You know your Paw Paw loves you." Danielle had made it downstairs because I could hear her saying, "Good morning Dorothy." This is how we would jokingly tell Mom and Dad good morning sometimes by saying their first name. She walked into the kitchen and I was looking out of the window. She asked me if I was okay, and I told her, "Yes, I'm just watching your Paw Paw trying to stay busy." I didn't know if she could tell that I had been crying, so I walked into the living room and just stood by the couch. When she was done in the kitchen, she walked past me to go back upstairs.

She stopped, put her hands on my shoulders and said, "This too will pass. We're going to be okay." But with tears in her eyes she said, "They ain't right. They both left me here by myself. Why did they do me like this?" She had a serious look on her face. She said, "For real though." With tears in her eyes, she chuckled a little bit. We would have a lot of those moments where you would laugh to keep from crying. I hugged her and told her that we were going to hurt and miss her. But with God and in time and that what she said was right, we were going to be okay. Her granny, brother and sister were most definitely going to be watching over her, also the boys, William and little William. She smiled and said, "I know, but they still ain't right."

About an hour had gone by, and we still weren't ready to go. It was like we were just going through the motions but getting nowhere fast. I think in our subconscious minds, we were stalling because though we believed in our hearts that her soul was already gone, we were in no hurry to see her in that state. In the meantime, my dad had come back into the house and was in his room watching TV. I walked past his room, and I could hear him crying. I walked in the room and put my arms around him. I told him that we were going to be alright and that she was safe in the arms of the Lord, and we wouldn't have to worry about her anymore. We were always worrying about her, because Yolanda was a free spirit. She didn't fear a lot of things like we did, and I think she may have worried daddy the most. Regardless of how old they were, Danielle was his big baby and Yolanda was his little baby, and you could always tell when he was concerned or hurting. It was a painful thing to see, but I kept hearing Yolanda telling me, "You have to be strong momma." I was in constant prayer for strength, and the Lord came through every time and gave me strength and peace of mind that passes all understanding. I was determined that the little bit of strength that I had in me was going to continue to give God the praise, honor and thanks. Why you might ask, because he blessed me with 21 years, and I could have lost her when she was just a week old. I could have been without both daughters and my grandsons. The Lord would keep reminding me to look at the positive things that were taking place and not to get caught up in the tragedy and the darkness that surrounded it. I had to remove myself from an earthly realm way of thinking and look at things in the spiritual realm. I will tell anybody that if you take refuge in the Lord, you will find him to be everything he promised. Trust him and stand on his promises for that's all I knew to do.

We finally got a phone call that would help us get a little pep in our step. Their dad had received a call from Kim at the hospital. She wanted to know if we were still allowing visitors, because someone was taking pictures. Her dad said he was in agreement with whatever we decided. I called her immediately to inform her that we were on our way. She told me there was no rush because her and my Aunt Rosie was security and they had everything under control. She asked the young lady to delete the picture, and she was very respectful and did so. She just wanted to know if only family was allowed and how long they could visit. I told her that Yolanda's friends could still visit, but only for a few minutes, no lingering in the room and no cell phones. She said, "No problem, we have it under control. See you when you get here." I didn't worry at all, because I knew that they had it under control. You would have to meet them both to know that they meant what they said.

The Journey Continued

We finally got in the car and headed to the hospital. We began talking about Yolanda and things she would do, laughing sometimes and fighting back tears at others. We reminisced on how Yolanda could do something and have you so mad at her. You couldn't stay mad at her for long, because she would do something silly and tell you to get over it. All you could do was laugh, shake your head, and she was back on your good side. While talking, we discovered that she had shared a dream with the both of us around February or March about death. I think that it really bothered her. Now that we were talking about it, we couldn't help but think if it was a sign. We finally reached the hospital and I got a spot right in front. I put the car in park, and we just looked at each other. As we were getting out of the car, a weight came over me. Once we entered the hospital and got on the elevator, my heart started pounding fast. I looked at Danielle and asked her if she was ok because I could imagine that she might be experiencing the same thing. We walked off the elevator into the intensive care unit. Yolanda was in room number 2, so you were right at her room as soon as you walked in. We walked into the room and to our surprise, the swelling had gone down some. You could actually see her eyes and nose. Though her face was still swollen, I could take it better at least being able to make out something. I walked over to the bed and began to rub her hand. Danielle walked around to the other side. We were talking to her, and then I saw Danielle's eyes fill with tears. So, I walked to the other side of the bed and put my arms around her, and we continued to talk. Then her dad walked in. He said, "Hey lil momma, hey child," as he walked to the foot of the bed and just looked at her with tears in his eyes.

    I said, "Well, the swelling has gone down some."

He said, "I see."

Just trying to lighten things up I said, "You can see her nose."

He said, "Watch out now, that's the Logan trademark you're talking about." We all smiled, and then he said his famous words when it came to Yolanda, "Dat Girl."

Kim stepped in while we were there just to let us know that she was there if we needed anything and that she would talk to us before we left. We didn't stay long because Kim had already let us know that she would be calling us back up to the hospital to do the paperwork for the organ donation later in the day. We stayed for 10 or 15 more minutes and then we left. We stopped by the room Kim was working out of, and she stepped out to talk to us. We laughed about her and my aunt having to play security, and then she went on to tell me about a young man that had come to visit Yolanda before we gotten there. She had let him stay for a while.

My Life Under the Sonshine | 63

She said that she felt his sincerity, and she could see the pain he was feeling. After she described him, I knew that it was an ex-boyfriend and I told her that it was fine. Then she said something that would help me to keep looking at the positive things that were taking place.

She said, "I don't know Yolanda, but yet I feel close to her. I wish that I had met her. The love that's being shown, you know that she was special. And as many as it was of you all, you weren't loud, being disrespectful. There was just praying and a humbled presence all around her. The Staff and I have been amazed at the fact that you are allowing people to visit her in this state, normally people want their privacy."

I had to let her know that Yolanda would want people to visit, because she would always take her most painful situations and use them as teachable moments.

She said, "I love it." Then she went on to tell us what to expect when she called us to come back to the hospital. We hugged and then we left. As we were walking back to our cars, William told me that he would pick me up so that I wouldn't have to drive back by myself. I was very grateful for that. Riding home, it was back to Yolanda stories. When we made it back to the house, it was quiet. My mom's sisters and my uncle Joe was there. People had brought food, drinks, desserts, toilet paper and paper towels. Yes, toilet paper, and I had never thought about that until she explained why. You always think to take food because you expect a lot of people might come. Well those same people may have to use the bathroom or wash their hands, it made so much sense. Anyway, no one really stayed, they were just dropping things off. It was a chance to chill before going back to the hospital. I couldn't sleep, so all I could do was try to enjoy my family's company and try not to overthink things. William called around 9 o'clock to inform me that Kim had called. She was ready for us to come to do the paperwork for the organ donation. He called my phone to let me know that he was outside. I get in the car and he says, "Hey lil momma, how are you doing?"

"I'm hanging in there," I said.

"I still can't believe this is happening, but it is." He goes on to let me know that he had contacted the funeral home, and we had an appointment at 1 o'clock on the 13th, which was Monday. It's getting even more real now because things are starting to happen.

We arrived at the hospital and went up to the intensive care unit. I looked into Yolanda's room and let her know that I would be back before we left. Kim was informed that we were there. She came out and greeted us with a big smile and hug. She escorted us into the room that set next to the nurse's station. She had to wait on a phone call. We talked and shared with one another. I can't even explain the atmosphere in the room. It was like God had brought us together at that moment in our lives because we had something to offer one another. After we had witnessed and bonded with one another, the phone call came. We proceeded with the paperwork. After we were done, Kim turns her chair and picks up a blue box off of the table behind her. She turns back around and begins to speak. I can't remember exactly but it went a little something like this: "On behalf of myself and KODA, we are sorry for your loss but we would like to give you a token of love and our appreciation for the selfless act that Yolanda has done. I know that you are proud of her, she is a Hero."

She reached back again, and she had 2 Christmas ornaments in her hand. She said, "We don't have medals for everyone, but we would also like to present you with these ornaments made by a recipient that wanted to show their appreciation to families of organ donors."

Right away we decided to give them to Danielle and Kennedi. William and I went on to say how proud we were of her. A chill came over me and I looked down at my phone, it was midnight. Officially Mother's Day, my eyes teared up. It was like her spirit had come into the room and I heard her say, "Happy Mother's Day Momma. See, I was everything you thought I should be."

It was like I was in the room for a second by myself. Then I heard Kim saying that she would give us a call in an hour before they took her down for the procedure if anyone wanted to come back to the hospital. We wrapped things up and stopped by the room. Her dad stood at the foot of the bed with tears in his eyes. and I went to my same spot. I told her thank you again and I was proud of her, but I also had to tell her

I was sorry. I knew that she had a heart of gold and what she was capable of, but I had gotten focused on all of the negative things. That was another eye-opening moment for me. There was nothing we could do, so we went home to wait for the phone call that we would be getting later in the day. By the time I got home, everyone was gone but my Aunt Linda. She was walking to her car when we pulled into the driveway. You could tell by the way she was walking that she was tired.

"Whoo child these bones are tired; I'll see you tomorrow." All I could do was laugh, because I really needed that. We all said goodnight. I walked into the house and everybody, but mom had gone to bed. I shared with her what happened at the hospital, showed her the medal and got ready for bed.

I opened my eyes the next day and it was Sunday morning. Of course, mom is already up getting ready for church. Daddy's outside getting the backyard ready for what he knows is about to be just the beginning of a house full of company coming and going all day. I lay there for a minute, thanking the Lord for another day. I told Yolanda good morning. I finally got out of bed and the doorbell rang. It was my aunt Linda stopping by to see if there was anything she could do before going to church. At the same time, the phone was ringing. People are calling to see if anybody would be home so that they could drop off food and calling with their condolences. My Aunt Linda got right on phone detail and doing whatever else she could do until she left for church.

All I could think to myself was, 'Ok here we go.' I went upstairs to check on Danielle and to get my clothes to put on for the day. Once I got back downstairs, I realized that I hadn't told my mom good morning. Before could say anything, with a big smile on her face, she hugged me and said, "Good morning beautiful daughter, today is still a good day. God makes no mistakes, she's alright and we're going to be alright."

I told her good morning and said, "Yes ma'am, I know that we are." I just love my mother's spirit. I got dressed and went outside to check on my dad. I could tell he had been crying. I asked him if he was ok. He just shook his head, made a little moaning sound and hugged me. I gave him that same assurance my mom had just given me. I think me and mom knew that we had to be strong for the family.

While outside, my cousin Carolyn stopped by on her way to church to drop off tents. Then her mom Joetta came with food and desserts. Then my cousin Debra came and they started to get the food and stuff situated. Jeannie, Kim, Catherine and Yolanda came next with more things, it was like a domino effect. Though they are my cousins, being an only child growing up around them, they are more like my brothers and sisters. They will never know the strength I received from the love and support they gave us during a very rough time. Danielle and Bless finally made their way downstairs. As I looked at him, I thought about the tattoo Yolanda had so boldly going across her chest that read Blessed.

I just thought to myself, 'She had broadcasted his arrival, her Virgo baby as she called him.' His life was just beginning as hers came to an end. He was bringing so much joy in the midst of sorrow. We could already see Yolanda in him which was funny. Now, it was getting close to time for people to get out of church and it hits me that we hadn't got the call to come to the hospital. It was going on 1 o'clock. I believe it was shortly after that when my phone made a beep. I picked it up and it was an inbox in messenger. It still wasn't Kim, but to my surprise it was someone reaching out to me about the accident. Her name was Heather Yocum. I can't remember everything the message said, but she stated that she was at the scene of the accident and she found me on Facebook. She included her number and asked if I would call her. Shaking, I went to Danielle and told her what had just happened.

She said, "For real? Call her, momma." I got myself together and called. A female picked up, I asked to speak to Heather, and it was her. I went on to introduce myself and thanked her for reaching out to me. She began to tell me that she couldn't understand why people were just standing around looking and wasn't trying to do anything to help them. She wanted me to know that she tried to do what she could for both Yolanda and her boyfriend. She went on to tell me that Yolanda was pent up in the car and she couldn't get her out. She talked to her until the ambulance got there letting her know that she was going to be alright and she wasn't alone. She stated that just being a mother herself, she would want to know that her child wasn't alone at a time like that. Trying to hold myself together, I thanked her for not only being Yolanda's angel but my family's angel as well. I let her know that Yolanda had passed and told her again, that she was an angel sent by God. I expressed how grateful I was that she stayed with her and comforted her as best she could until the ambulance arrived. She gave her condolences and said that she was no angel and far from being a saint. She didn't know at the time that mom and I had discussed the accident earlier before she went to church. We were questioning what she must have been going through. Was she conscious? We were praying that she didn't have to experience a lot of pain and about the fact that no one was able to be there with her through that hurt. So, she was an angel sent by God to stand in my place as a mother and to answer our concerns. We vowed to keep in touch with one another so that we could meet face to face. As soon as I got off of the phone, I went to tell Danielle. It was like a sense of relief. I couldn't wait for mom to get home to tell her.

It's going on 3 o'clock and we were ready. Chairs had been set out in the house and the backyard is ready for whoever wanted to be outside. I can remember my Uncle Joe and my Aunts Viola, Sarah and Linda being the first to pull up. Before long, we had a house full of folk. The older set was inside. Danielle and Yolanda's age group were gathering outside. I was all over the place just trying to stay busy. There were plenty of food, drinks and desserts, but they were still coming. Lee Ann had even brought Yolanda's favorite tea that she would purchase from her after church on Sundays.

She said, "I had to bring my girls tea. She loved my tea." All I could do was smile, because Yolanda could have made her a commercial.

Whenever she bought some home, she would come in with the little jug smacking her lips, being so dramatic.

"Momma you have to try it, this tea is fa," then she'd drink some and start twerking or something, she was such an actress. It was those moments that brought about laughter and reminiscence that soothed the pain that you were feeling for the moment. It was the love that was being shown for Yolanda and my family that gave me more strength. Though I was being comforted by seeing family and friends coming together laughing, sharing old stories and new, I was still on an emotional roller coaster. Every time the phone rang, I was reminded that I was waiting on that phone call. It was going on 5 o'clock and still no call. I began to feel overwhelmed, so I went upstairs to be alone for a moment. I had a talk with the Lord, cried and got myself together and then went outside for a minute. I didn't stay long because I didn't want to make them feel uncomfortable with me being out there. Shortly after that, Danielle, my cousins that were Yolanda's age and a few of Yolanda's friends came into the house. They surprised me with cards, flowers and a teddy bear. They all said things that brought me to tears and then we had a group hug. As they all put their arms around me, not only could I feel their love, but I could feel my baby's presence. I put the flowers and cards on the table with the medal and took a picture. That really caught me off guard. I had so much on my mind, that I hadn't even thought about it being Mother's Day.

It was later in the day, and I finally got the call that I've been waiting for only for Kim to tell me that they wouldn't be doing the procedure until Monday. She felt so bad, but I understood that she had no control over how things were going. I held my composure while I was on the phone, but once I hung up, I just broke down crying.

Danielle came and asked me what was wrong. All I could say with tears streaming down my face, "Why are they playing with my emotions? Nobody's been to the hospital today, because we were waiting on the phone call. I'm just ready for it to be over with."

Danielle put her arms around me and with a smile on her face asked me if I needed a hug.

Still crying and laughing at the same time, I said, "Yes."

Then in a calm voice she says, "Momma, it's been a good day. It's late, and we have a house full of people. It wouldn't be right for you to leave now, there's nothing we can do. I think Yolanda understands and would want us to wait until tomorrow."

The fact that I had been trying to stay strong for her and to see her being the voice of reason at my weakest point, just made it visible to me that God was going to get us through this. I went upstairs and had a moment to myself, talked to Yolanda and went back downstairs. People had been coming, going and it finally started clearing out around 9:30-10:00. Once again, my Aunt Linda was the last to leave. After I had finally settled down, got in bed and it was quiet, I was able to see what God had done. He had held the procedure up, so that I wouldn't have to remember Mother's Day in the future going to the hospital to see her for the last time before they took her down for the procedure and the funeral home picking her up. Instead, I would have the memory of receiving the medal, ornaments, flowers, cards and the conversation with Heather, laughter and the acts of love that was shown during the day.

It's Monday morning, I opened my eyes and thanked the Lord for another day. I said good morning Yodie. I got out of bed and the doorbell rings. I opened the door and it's my Aunt Linda standing there with a big smile on her face, "Secretary reporting for duty," laughing as she entered the house. I couldn't help but shake my head and laugh along with her. I am so grateful for the energy that she brought every morning. She showed up every morning at the same time. She wouldn't leave until the last person was gone home that night. I know that Yolanda was probably looking down on us smiling and in shock. See my Aunt Linda, better known as Aunt Moot, is that no nonsense type of person. I think everybody has one or two, because my Aunt Viola runs a close 2nd. Everybody knows it's all love. She'll have you cracking up one minute and walking on cotton the next. Seeing her every morning made me think back to when Yolanda was much younger and how she went to stay over at her house along with her twin cousins that were her age.

They never wanted to go back, and my Aunt would laugh and say, "that's fine by me."

I just smiled and said, "Yodie, your Aunt Moot is showing out for you."

I began to get dressed for my day so that I would be ready when the call came to come to the hospital and for our meeting with the funeral home to make the arrangements. Everyone is starting to move around. Dad was out back trying to stay busy as usual. He eventually came in, and as he's walking past me, he catches me off guard and hugs me.

When he releases me, I said, "Albert, are you alright, because just about every time you walk past me, you're grabbing me?" I smiled.

With his voice quivering he says, "I'm sorry, I just don't think I've handed out enough of them., God knows I loved her. I love all of yaw. I just wish I could tell her how much I love her. I wish there was something I could have done."

Now, we're both standing there with tears in our eyes. I assured him that she knew that he loved her. We had figured out that he just had a weird way of showing it.

I looked up towards heaven and said, "Thank you Lord. I see what you're doing, and I'm going to keep standing on your promise."

My father has never really been an affectionate person. There were times in my life that I needed a hug from him and I didn't get it. For him to live long enough to recognize that, and for me to live long enough to receive the affection and hear him say that, was such a blessing. That healed many wounds from over the years. I had already been seeing growth in my father since he had gotten back into church, but I could see that Yolanda's passing was getting ready to take it to another level. True enough, it's a sad time, but I could see God.

Around 11 o'clock, William calls and says we have an hour to get to the hospital before they take her to have the procedure done. I get on the phone and call everyone that said they wanted to be there. I let Danielle know, but she had changed her mind about going.

"I can't do it momma; I just can't do it." I had to be strong for her, just as she had been strong for me earlier. I told her that Yolanda understood. She wasn't there anyway and that was just the shell that housed her soul. We were just going to have prayer. She wouldn't want her getting on the road all messed up, because they were leaving later that day so that she could get back to work. Mom and I got ready to head to the hospital. Once we got there and walked into the room, we realized that more swelling had gone down. As we waited to make sure no one else was coming, we just talked, laughed, rubbed her hands and told Yolanda stories. Several family members had shown up, including Reverend Nikki Wharton. She's an associate minister at Cable Baptist Church where I grew up, but where Yolanda and William currently attended.

She would have the last Yolanda story. She began to talk about a Sunday where Yolanda had gotten happy during Sunday service about two months before the accident. She went on to say that everyone in the church was shouting, having a good time and from nowhere this little woman came flying down the isles from the balcony. She went on to say that she didn't even think that she had walked down the steps, so she must have flown. Before she knew it, she was down in front of the church, dancing around with people including the pastor and the guest speaker. My Aunt Rosie chimed in, "I remember that. One minute, she was clapping in the balcony, then you didn't see her anymore because she was in the front of the church.

Her dad spoke up, "Yeah I remember that. She had her a good time, "Dat Girl." I just smiled, because I remembered that Sunday as well. Not because I was at the service, but she had come home from church so excited.

She came in floating on a cloud saying, "Mama, I feel so good. No for real, I feel good. I got happy in church today. I don't know what happened. I was up in the balcony and the next thing I know I'm in the Pulpit dancing with the preacher. I was dancing with anybody I saw. I'm on a high and I ain't coming down, I'm staying away from all negative energy today, ain't nothing or nobody gonna bother me today."

I smiled and said, "It sounds like to me you were doing the square dance."

We both laughed and then she said, "I don't care what I was doing or how it looked, all I know is I feel good, and Mama I let it all go."

I was so happy for her and to hear her say that, because she had been carrying so much weight for so long. To finally know that she had let it go, I could have shouted myself. I had to let her know that I knew exactly how she felt and that it's the best feeling ever, to be free. As she was bouncing around the house getting ready to leave, I reminded her not to let anybody steal her joy. That was another moment I could reflect and see God. After that, Reverend Wharton lead us in prayer and we said see you later once again.

As we were leaving the hospital, William realized it was almost time for our appointment with the funeral home. Mom rode back to the house with my Uncle Joe and my Aunt Viola. When we got to the funeral home, we were a little early. I got in his car and we talked for a minute. He went on to remind me that this was about to be the hardest part.

I'm thinking to myself; 'How could this be the hardest part?' Seeing my baby laying there in that bed, knowing that she wasn't coming back, how could this be the hardest part? We walked into the funeral home. Miss Linda was working in the office who was a member of my mom's Church. She led us to another room and told us someone would be with us shortly. While we waited, William just talked to me about different things because he had already experienced it. The funeral director came in, we talked for a minute and then it was down to business. She began to ask us questions about what we wanted, pallbearers, what date we were trying to have the funeral and the program.

I'm thinking to myself, 'This is not hard at all.' Then she brought out the book with the caskets in it. I'm still thinking to myself this is not going to be hard because I already knew what color she wanted. When I selected the casket and said this is the one I want, I just started crying. I finally understood what William meant. We had been through all the other things and this was the final act that she was gone and never coming back. They gave me a minute to get myself together and then we wrapped everything up. She informed me that I would have to get whatever she would be wearing and the program back as soon as possible.

Thinking that the worst part of my day was over, I headed home to spend time with Danielle and the kids before they got on the road to go home. I pulled into my driveway, and my phone rang. It was one of the nurses from the hospital asking me if I wanted to pick up Yolanda's belongings.

I'm thinking to myself, 'Are you serious? I thought I was done with the hospital. What could they have?' I tell the nurse that I'll come back. I went into the house to let everyone know where I was going. Danielle asked me if I wanted her to ride with me and I told her that I would be okay going by myself. Once I get there, the nurse goes to the back and comes back with a plastic hazardous bag. I can see that there's money in it, so I asked her if there was any blood on it because I didn't want to see it.

She looked at it and said, "No." I took it and headed back to my car. While I was riding up Broadway, I decided to take it out of the bag to see how much it was, because I knew that she was supposed to pay her rent. When I took it out it was ok on the outside, but when I unfold it, it had blood on the money inside. I threw it back in the bag and broke down crying. I pulled into the driveway, went straight to the backyard and laid the money out on the concrete and started spraying it with the water hose. Dad came out and asked what I was doing. When I told him, he shook his head and went back into the house. By the time Danielle came out, I was done, I had gotten the blood off all of it but one bill. They were about to start loading up to get on the road. I counted the money. She had $260.00 on her, and she hadn't made to the house to get what I had left her.

I could just hear her saying, "Give it to Danni," so I gave it to her.
She said, "Momma are you sure?"
I told her, "Yes, your sister would want you to have it." She counted and started crying, this is just about what I needed for a bill.
She said, "Thank you Lord, Thank you, Yolanda, You're looking out for your sister."

We thought about something Yolanda would have said and had to laugh. They finished putting stuff in the car, said goodbye and loaded up to head home. I felt so bad for her. I was going to have the support of family and friends, and she was going to be 6 hours away having to deal with her accident and all of those other emotions by herself.

It's Tuesday morning, and my Aunt shows up like clockwork with a big smile and laughing. I knew that the house was going to be quiet until later on in the day because Danielle and the boys were gone. I didn't want to just sit around and let my mind start to wander. It had been suggested that I needed to go check on her apartment. I had already called the rent office on Saturday and let the manager know what happened. It was just a matter of me letting her know when I wanted to get the key. I made the call, and she told me that I could come on and get the key. I didn't want to go alone, so my cousins Dyiun and Darrick went with me. I met the manager when Yolanda first got the apartment. She was so excited. She wanted me to be with her when she signed her lease. That was a big moment for the both of us. I was so proud of her. There was another occasion when Yolanda had a question about her lease, and she wanted me with her. When I walked into her office, both of our eyes just filled with tears.

She said, "I am so sorry. I have lost other residents, but this is hitting me hard."

She was so sweet, and I could tell she was trying so hard. It was just something about her, it was her smile. Every time she came into the office, she had the prettiest smile. I thanked her for giving Yolanda the opportunity and for just helping her with any questions or concerns she may have had. Though it only lasted 5 months, that was a big moment in her life to have her own place. She gave me the key, hugged me and told me there was no rush. When we walked into the apartment, I got really sad because I started thinking about how excited she was that it was summer. She was going to let the kids spend the night and go swimming. She also wanted to have a family game night. I got a little mad because I had only been there 4 times and 2 of those times I pulled up and didn't go in. I felt cheated. I was mad at myself for always working and not changing shifts way before I did, it wasn't fair. I didn't let it show, but I couldn't take being in there, so we didn't stay long. I just looked around to see what was going to have to be done, and then we left. By the time I made it home, I received a call from Danielle that brightened my day. She went into work and they told her she didn't need to be there. They would work things out when she came back to work. She would be coming back to Louisville before Friday. Hearing that made me feel a whole lot better. We agreed to go to the mall on Thursday to get Yolanda's outfit. All I had left to do was drop the obituary off to Miss Linda. After that, it would be sitting around the house waiting to see who would be stopping by.

I didn't mind the company because it kept my mind off of things.

It's Wednesday morning, and it gets started the same. I thank the Lord for another day and say God Morning Yodie. I texted Danielle and the boys, told them good morning and that I loved them as I did every day. There was somewhat of a void there, even though I was telling Yolanda good morning. I was used to texting her every morning and telling her that I loved her, and then I would get a response. Before I could drift off to a dark place, my Aunt shows up with her laugh and happy energy reporting for duty. I got myself together because I had a few things to do. First stop was picking up the obituary and memory cards from the funeral home. Yolanda was a U of K fan, so we chose to have a blue and white carnation spray to sit on the casket with blue and white U of K ribbons. Of course, the obituary had to be U of K. We knew she would have wanted it that way.

When I picked them up, I just glanced at it, right away you could see that smile and those deep dimples, it was perfect. Next stop was to drop off the T-shirts at Good Fellows. Stacy Biggers, a longtime friend of the family wanted to do something for the family, so she paid for everyone's shirt. My last stop was going back to the apartment. I made arrangements to meet my best friend Shenigua to begin gathering whatever things I could get into my car. Before heading that way, I stopped by the house to drop off the obituary and memory cards. I sat in the car for a minute, I picked up the obituary to read it and my heart dropped. I had been so drawn in by her smile on the picture that I hadn't noticed that the picture that I chose her arms were bare, and you could see the tattoo with my name on it that she had gotten the year before. I hadn't even noticed it until then. Once we made it to the apartment, I headed for the kitchen and my friend said that she would start bagging up her clothes. I was so grateful for her helping me, especially getting the clothes together. I wouldn't have been able to do it by myself. I'm in the kitchen and she's in the bedroom, so it's quiet for a minute. I started to think about how she always had me laughing. When she first got the apartment, she didn't have cable. The TV that I gave her had a DVD player on it, but for some reason it only played Friday out of all of the movies she had. She would call me cussing and complaining. I would be cracking up, and she couldn't help but laugh at herself. I was going to get her a bigger one for her birthday. She called me excited one day because she had got Cable. I couldn't help but smile. Then I heard Sheniqua saying something from the bedroom. I asked her what she said. She replied, "I was just telling Yolanda that Auntie was about to have an asthma attack, it's hot as hell in here."

I told her, "Please don't do that," and we both laughed. I thanked God for the laughter because it changed the atmosphere. We got everything out except the big stuff, but I wasn't going to worry about that until after the funeral.

By the time I made it home, there were people already there. I walked into the house and broke down. The first person I saw was my cousin Lisa from Huntsville. When I tell you that I love my cousins so much, rather they live near or far. Whether I see them all of the time or hardly see them at all, they mean the world to me. Just seeing her sitting there and she told me that my cousin Geraldine was there, words can't explain. Later in the day, I would have another surprise visit. My friend Yolanda, who named me godmother of her daughter LaShay and her sister Nesha came through the door. I was so glad to see them, because I had lost contact with them and hadn't seen them in years. Only to find out that Yolanda had been in contact with LaShay and Nesha, but for some reason, that didn't surprise me. Shay was my baby; I had her all of the time. My baby wasn't a baby anymore.

She was expecting a little one of her own. It had been a busy and exciting day. It ended on a good note because Danielle, Haiti and the boys made it back to Louisville safely.

It's Thursday morning, I wake up and do the usual and proceed to get ready for our day at the mall. All I could think about was if we were going to be able to find something blue with a white shawl or sweater. Once we were both ready, we headed to the mall to one of Yolanda's favorite stores. We couldn't believe what we were about to do, but it had to be done. We walked into the store and saw a couple of dresses right away, we picked the one we felt Yolanda would choose, that was easy, but we couldn't find a sweater or shawl. Thank goodness a family member had one. We were done. I dropped Danielle off at the house because she had something to do and I took the clothes to the funeral home. The director told me everything was fine and I headed back home.

It's Friday, and it's pretty much a chill day. All that needed to be done was, pick up the T-shirts, and go to the viewing at 6 o'clock. At least, that's what we thought. Any family members or friends that wanted to attend the viewing already knew what time to be there, so we were just waiting. Then at around 4 o'clock, we get a call from the funeral home. Yolanda's outfit was too small. They thought that they could make it work, but they just couldn't do it. It's 2 hours before the viewing and she has nothing to wear. She told me to find something with long sleeves if possible and nothing cut to low, but if it was, get a scarf. We were told the bigger the better, they could always make it fit. I began to panic, but Danielle calmed me down. Heading to the malls wasn't an option because there was no time for that. We headed out Dixie Hwy, walked into the store and every dress we saw, was made on the order of the dress we already had. Right when Danielle told me to come on, we needed to go somewhere else, something told me to go to the back of the store. I told her to hold on, I crossed the isles, cut through the racks and headed to the back. I ended up in the plus size section. Setting on the rack right in front of me, the other dresses that were pushed back to where I couldn't miss it. A Kentucky blue, long sleeve dress. I couldn't believe it; it was almost scary. I picked it up and walked back to Danielle.

She said, "Where did you find that?"

I'm looking at her like, I don't know what just happened. I don't know if it was God, or if Yolanda's spirit is that strong, but that's why I told you to wait. Something told me to go to the back of the store, and I went right to it. It wasn't cut low, but we looked for a white scarf just in case. We couldn't find one, but we did find an earring and necklace set, purchased it and headed to the next store. We ended up out Cane Run Rd, walked into the store and found one. We didn't really like it, so we headed across the lot to Walmart, and saved that one for a last result. Walked into to Walmart and went to the purses section and walked to the rack where they kept the scarfs. It happened again, sitting right there in our faces like it was waiting on us, the perfect white scarf. We look at each other, Danielle grabbed the scarf and we headed for the checkout line. We got in the car and we couldn't believe it, in less than an hour we had everything we needed. Coincidence I think not, we both agreed that was nothing but God. I dropped her off at the house so that she could get dressed and I headed for the funeral home. I was over it.

I hadn't received any phone calls, so I assumed that everything was alright. Finally, it was time to head to the viewing. Daddy didn't want to go because he didn't know how she would look. I understood because he was already taking it hard. I could see that it was bothering him. I assured him that it was alright and we all understood because that was his little baby. Some of our family were already there waiting. We all walked into the funeral home. Miss Linda greeted us at the door and proceeded to walk us down the hallway where she was. It was a short walk but yet it seemed so long. She opened the door, and right away I could see her features from the side. As we're walking in, the tears started falling. Danielle was talking to her and tears were rolling down the cloth that covers the casket. Mom and Aunt Bonnie were handing out tissues. I'm thankful that more of the swelling had gone down, because I think it would have been so much harder to handle. Daddy would have been alright, but I had Michele take her picture so that daddy could see her. They did a good job. I told them how she liked to have her baby hair laying down and they had it just right. You're standing there looking at her but a part of you is still saying this can't be happening. I'm about to bury my baby. Miss Linda stuck her head in the door to check on us. I asked if we could have a little more time because my goddaughter Kennedi had just got in town, and she was on her way. She said that it was ok. Kennedi and her Aunt Candyce finally made it. She broke down when she walked in. I'm so grateful to God that her and Danielle both had been home more than they ever had. They both even made it out to her new apartment. I know that they weren't thinking about that at the time, but God just kept showing me the blessings beyond the tragedy. Miss Linda checked on us again, and we were just hanging around like we didn't have to leave.

    I walked over next to her, and in a soft whisper I said, "I know you say I'm lame, you're right and I'm sorry, but I'm going to sing you a song." I started to sing, His Eye Is On The Sparrow, a few joins in, and then her dad said a prayer. After seeing her, we didn't know if we wanted to do open or closed casket, so we told her goodbye while we could see her just in case. Afterwards, everyone met back at the house.

It's Saturday morning, and today we take my baby to her resting place. It was a beautiful day, the sun was shining, and spirits seemed to be high considering the circumstances. I woke up feeling blessed, just thinking about all of the things that had taken place up to that moment. I was blessed to have had two beautiful daughters and two handsome grandsons. The fact that I was about to say see you later to Yolanda, was well with my soul. God keeps his promise to dry my tears, never leave me nor forsake me, he walked with me and talked with me all week long. God told me to have hope and not to grieve as if I would never see her again. I woke up with hope and with a heart of gratitude. Was I emotional? Yes, I was, but I was grateful for the 21 years. Grateful that I had a chance to see her have some happy days and accomplish some things that she wanted to accomplish.

Grateful to know that she was connected to the main power source, grateful and at peace because God had assured me, that though she was absent from the body, she would be with Him. I was still standing on His promises, giving Him the praise and giving satan nothing.

Everybody got dressed, William and his wife Estell and two of her family members came to the house. The funeral cars arrived, we got in the cars and headed to the church. We did not understand the magnitude of the love, support and the impact Yolanda had made on the lives of young and old alike until we walked into that church. There was support there for the family as well. I had so many people to hug me and tell me how much they loved Yolanda and the impact she made on their lives. I couldn't even cry. I stood there next to her casket, strong and so proud to be her mother. She always told us that we didn't know her, but we were learning more about her on that day. It added to how proud of her I already was. Two of Yolanda's elementary school teachers came to the wake, Mr. Lightsy and Ms. Ballenghar. She gave them a run for their money, but I don't know if they ever knew how much she thought of them. Being there meant a lot. I did tear up when I saw Shannon walking down the aisles. We shared such a deep concern for Yolanda because of what she had experienced. and Yolanda and I both knew that she loved her very much. I treasured every hug, because Yolanda loved to hug. I felt like every hug was not only from them but from her as well. As it came to the end of the wake, we were faced with making the decision to leave the casket closed or open it for the family to view only as we processioned in. Antonio would give us the answer. It hadn't hit him until near the end of the wake that she was gone and never coming back. He gave me and his mother the biggest scare.

Danielle quickly said, "Momma, I'm not going to be able to take it. I'm trying my best to hold up. I won't be able to handle people falling out all over the place."

We decided to leave it closed and once we knew that Antonio was alright, Yolanda's step-sister volunteered to take him away from the church. We went back upstairs, and it was so crowded. The family was scattered everywhere, so we decide not to walk in. We just went into the Home going.

There were tears shed, but it was a celebration of her life, the legacy of love and selflessness she left behind. Every minister that spoke before the eulogy played a part in her life, and that smile and energy had left an impact. Her cousin Dominique got up and spoke. He was always on her case like a big brother. He spoke some powerful words that I prayed wouldn't fall on deaf ears. He made her proud.

She didn't want a choir or soloist, so I honored her wishes. Mom had selected the song, Except What God Allows. I selected one of her favorite songs, 'I Pray We'll All Be Ready.' When it started playing, I couldn't help but think about how we had just sung it together about two weeks before the accident. When it got to her favorite part, I turned around to those sitting behind us and let them know that was her favorite part. By the time I turned back around, I could hear the church singing along with the recording.

I raised my arms and just started praising God, I said, "Yodie, do you hear that, it sounded beautiful." The atmosphere that was in that church. Pastor Middleton spoke the Eulogy that caused a shift in the atmosphere to an even higher level. He even mentioned the Sunday she got happy in church that made us smile. As he ended his sermon, he gave the invitation. A group of her friends came down for prayer. We didn't want to walk out on one of the traditional songs. We wanted it to be something that fit her. William chose 'Smile,' and as we stood up to leave the church and the song started to play. I was walking down the aisles and I could just imagine the smile on her face. It was a celebration, but it didn't stop there. Once we got to the cemetery and the benediction was given, Chase said a few words and released the balloons. As I was walking back to the car, I could see family members that hadn't been speaking hugging and talking. When you look beyond the tragedy, it was a good day.

It's days later, and I have to get my mind wrapped around going to get the big items out of the apartment and turn the keys in to the office. I got some folk together and we went and got everything else out. As we were loading the truck, the guy that lived across from her came out and asked was she moving. He hadn't seen her. She usually greeted him every morning with a smile and with telling him good morning. I let him know that she passed away. He gave his condolences and said she was always smiling. Knowing how Yolanda was, I asked him if he wanted anything from the apartment. He was able to use a few things that made me feel good, because she was still giving. We cleared everything out except a little table and the middle section to her dinette table, which we gave to her friend Dontay. I figured once they went into the storage closet and seen it, hopefully someone could use it. We went through all of the closets and rooms to make sure we had everything out. The rent office had already closed, so I was going to have to turn the key in on the next day. Different people took certain things, so everything was dropped off where it needed to go. I woke up the next day and got my day started. I made a few phone calls, and then headed to the apartment to turn in the key. Right when I was getting ready to pull up at the office to turn in the key, Dontay called me and told me that he wanted the middle section to the table. I told him he called just in time. I went back to the apartment, though it was empty, I walked around one more time just thinking again about the plans she had for the summer. Something drew me into the bedroom, as I was about to head out of the bedroom, something in my spirit said look at the closet door. As I looked, I could see something, but I couldn't make out what it was. As I got closer, I could tell it was a bracelet. It was a brown and white bracelet with a copper heart.

I just looked up and said, "Thank you and I love you too."

Some may not believe, but I see God and the spirit of Yolanda. If Dontay hadn't called when he did, I wouldn't have had a reason to go back to the apartment. Then to be drawn to the room and find the bracelet. The bedroom had been checked but I just believe in my heart that it was meant for me to find. This took me back to the day in the hospital when my uncle said that Yolanda's spirit was strong. I couldn't agree with him more.

The bracelet found on the door knob.

Peace Through Analogies

God came to me with what I want to call analogies, to bring a sense of peace, serenity, and understanding to my soul. And though my heart was shattered, he began to put the pieces back together again little by little. At the end, I would like to share a scripture that only He could have led me to, giving me confirmation that she was safe with him.

I will be honest, I am not a bible scholar, teacher…, but I do believe that if you open your heart and receive what he may be trying to say to you, He will give you understanding. I believe that God can convey a message to you through the Holy Spirit. A Lot of times when I read the scriptures, all I can do is go wow, because it fits a particular time or situation. After I began to write this chapter this scripture came to me, Habakkuk 2: 2-3. I was compelled to read the whole chapter, and I encourage whoever's reading this book to do the same. After reading verses 2 and 3, all I could say was, yes Lord, I'll try my best to write it in a way that people will understand and be able to carry it on and hopefully help others.

The puzzle, imagine God is working on this big beautiful puzzle. When you open the box, it consists of many pieces, different shapes, sizes and colors. I imagine that before you open the box, you look at the picture to see what the end result should look like. In the beginning, there's just a bunch of pieces, but as you begin to put the puzzle together and the pieces begin to thin out, you start to see a picture.

Most people start with the border first, and then start to fill in the middle. Sometimes you have pieces that you can just look at and tell right away where they go. There are other pieces that may be stuck together and you just place them within the border of the puzzle and add to them as you go along. There are pieces that you may have to turn around, around, and around trying to get it to fit. Sometimes you might get it, but there are times that you have to set it to the side and wait awhile. You may have some defective pieces. If they're not too bad, you place them if you can. If they are bad, you set them to the side until the end. At the end of the day, all of the pieces lie waiting, not knowing when their piece will be picked up and added to the puzzle.

Let's just say that the border pieces are those souls that are miscarried, aborted, still born and those whose lives were cut short before it really began. They too have a place in God's puzzle. Because the border is already started to be laid out, you have those pieces that you can tell right away where they go. Those are the souls that for whatever reason pass on at an early age. There are those pieces that you have to flip and turn different ways to try to get them to fit. Those are the souls that get to experience the ups and downs, good and bad, happy and sad times of life. Sometimes it takes a while to lay those pieces down, so you just sit them to the side until a better time. There are different colors in a puzzle, some dark, some light, some mixed with both, some are even blank just filling in a space. All of these pieces together are the souls of God's creation.

    The moral of it is, in the beginning of the puzzle, we're all just a bunch of scattered pieces. It doesn't matter when, where, or what took place for your puzzle piece to be laid. What's important is not the material gains or prestige that you may have obtained in the world, but what transpires from the time your existence began, until your puzzle piece is picked up and placed where God sees fit. When that day comes, no man, woman, boy, or girl will know the time, day or circumstances of their last moments. It could be tragic, due to illness, you could go to sleep and not wake up. Whatever the case may be, we may not want to think about it, but we all have an appointed time to take our rest. I've learned that what's important is the impact your life makes in the earthly realm, that uplifts and gives glory to God and the spiritual realm. Will your puzzle piece bring darkness to the world? Will it bring light in the midst of that darkness, or will it just be a blank piece?

Let me try to explain the puzzle pieces. You have the dark pieces and their purpose is to bring turmoil and chaos to the world. They are also all about earthly gain. They're not even trying to change or do better. They love being the way they are. You have the pieces that are a mixture of both darkness and light, and that's the majority of the puzzle. They are in a constant struggle or battle not to fall into the darkness. They have a desire and hope for better days and a better place, so they continue to fight through the warfare of this world. Then you have those pieces that have a little more color. They have been through the fire, but made it out. They are a testimony of God's grace and mercy. You can see it in their walk and hear it in their talk. They are a witness to all of the other pieces that there is a true and living God. At the end of the day, whatever part you play in this puzzle of life, God created us all.

I learned so much from this analogy. God's ways are not our ways. His thoughts are not our thoughts. He does not judge us as our sins deserve. I learned how really judgmental I can be. Yolanda's passing opened my eyes to the fact that God can use whomever He wants, when and however He chooses to do it. It's really none of my business. He doesn't really need my help other than to do the things He asked me to do. Though I loved her with all of my heart and only wanted to ease her pain and wanted the best for her, I had forgotten that God loved her more. He knew what He was doing. It would take for my baby's puzzle piece to be laid for me to see that I was so focused on all of the darkness around her, that I couldn't see the light she was bringing in the midst of that darkness. When I looked to God for understanding, He blinded me from the tragedy, chaos and darkness that surrounded her. God showed me that He was always with her and working through her. She was a diamond in the rough.

We are all apart of God's puzzle. It is not for us to think that we have all of the answers, nor should we pass judgement and think that we know who will and who will not enter into heaven. Sometimes we are only trying to save people from making the same mistakes we have made. There are times that we forget and must remember that we were once there ourselves. God is putting this puzzle together and He knows each piece one by one. He knows the picture that He's looking for. He will lay down the pieces as He sees a need to get to that perfect finish. He is fully aware of the powers that be that are working against us and Him. We must remember that everything that the devil means for bad, God has the power to work it out for our good whether in life and unto death. So it comes down to this, there is good and bad, happy times and sad, tragedy and chaos, life and death taking place in the midst of the puzzle. What will you bring to the puzzle? Only God truly knows our hearts. I pray that my light will shine before men and God gets the Glory.

Let me encourage those that are trying, but no one seems to notice and always has something to say. I am guilty as charged. Sometimes you have to encourage yourself and keep moving forward regardless of what people may say or think. Things will happen in God's time, not theirs. If you stumble and fall, get knocked down or get off track, that's alright. Get back up, dust yourself off and try again. The victory is in never giving up and fighting until your last breath. The race is not given to the swift but to the one that endures unto the end. When that end shall come you will hear him say, "Well done my good and faithful servant, you have fought the good fight." (In Yolanda's voice)

Parents, family members and friends, be careful of what you say or do. Things may look bad to you, but there is more than likely a bigger picture that only God can see. I can say that with confidence now, God knows all about it. Once you plant the seed of faith, hope, and love, nurture it as best you can, and believe that God will give the increase. Regardless of what you see with the human eye, sometimes it's not about them, it's more so about you or someone around you. With a sincere heart, ask God for understanding, and be open to receive what He might show you rather it be good or bad. Sometimes I believe God allows things to happen with hopes that it will help you, not hurt you. Trust in the Lord with all your heart, lean not unto your own understanding. He knows all about your concerns and He is in control.

The second analogy would be the caterpillar. We all know what eventually takes place with a caterpillar, and the same thing will happen with us. We will all go through our day by day regimens, but then one day a metamorphosis will start to take place, (the transition). We will one day began to come out of what Yolanda would call our sin skin. Once we've shed the sin skin, we will do as the butterfly. We will take flight and fly away, leaving behind all of those things that kept us bound. Heartache, sickness, sorrow, struggles and pain. We will have wings and soar high into the sky, doing what it says in my favorite scripture. (Philippians 3:13-14)

When God put the analogy of the butterfly in my spirit, I had to step out of my sorrow and let Him minister to me. I began to think about things that had taken place before the accident, conversations we had, happy and sad moments that we shared. There were days in the months prior to the accident that I would just get all of these songs in my spirit. I would listen to them and cry. Now that I look back, those songs were ministering to my soul in advance. Songs like Hold Back The Night, Send Your Spirit Lord, God Is A Good God, just to name a few. I saw God and so many things that I began to understand that she was going through her metamorphosis stage. I had witnessed her growth in so many ways, in her mind set and her spiritual life. All I could say was fly high my beautiful butterfly. I began to find even more peace in the midst of the sorrow .

The scripture that I was directed to was 1st Thessalonians 4:13-18. Because I have that hope, I can find joy in the midst of my sorrow. I know that one day, I will fly away and I will see her again .

Life Beyond Tragedy

Life since the accident hasn't been bad. I can honestly say that I've had more good days than bad days. I miss Yolanda very much and still have those days that I wish she was here getting on my nerves. But even in her absence, she continues to impact my life in so many ways. I still tell her good morning every morning, as I did when she was here with me. To me, that one day will never amount to the days that I had the opportunity to tell her Good Morning and that I loved her. We continue to have conversations, and she visits from time to time in ways that I know it's her. I had an encounter with a butterfly one day. I'm so glad my mom witnessed it. The following day, my goddaughter Kennedi had a similar experience. As I said before, you have to believe it to receive it. So, many things have happened since that day that are beyond coincidence. I continue to seek refuge in the

Almighty. He continues to give me strength and show me new mercies each day.

I wrote this book for many reasons. Although, I had to revisit some painful moments, it was therapeutic. I was reminded of blessings that have taken place along the way. In a conversation I had with Yolanda months later, she told me to live more, listen more, and love more. I didn't understand it then, but things have taken place since then that makes me try to do all three to the best of my ability. I can see growth in myself, Danielle, and in the broken family relationships. Jim, Theresa and Jary are like family and Yolanda is the reason for that connection. I'm grateful for the connection that I continue to have with Yolanda's closest friends. I'm grateful for being reunited with my goddaughter Lashay and the birth of her son coming at a time that I needed joy. He was born very early. He tried to come on Yolanda's birthday, but the doctor stopped her labor. He was born on September the 23rd. You would never know now that he was born premature and that's a blessing. It wasn't the 22nd, but we know better. I told his mom that he gets to celebrate two birthdays. I get to celebrate the life of two people that I love, one easing the pain of the other, if that makes sense. I'm blessed to be a part of the KODA Family Coalition. I have made friendships with some beautiful people. I'm doing things that I probably never would have done. I am humbled because I have been able to witness the sovereignty and grace of God.

I wrote this book because I want parents to understand that although we love our children with all of our hearts, we can make mistakes. Sometimes because we want what's best for them, but we can get in the way of what God's purpose is for them. I want parents to understand that mental health is important. We can't just allow our kids to be labeled and put on medications, possibly covering up a deeper issue. Counseling helped Yolanda in so many ways. It also helped me, and it strengthened our relationship because I was able to understand her better. People think that you're considered crazy if you go to get help, but there is nothing wrong with loving yourself enough to want to get control and a better grip on your life. There are people that have been blessed with the gift to help, I'm a witness.

I wrote this book because I want people to see that it's not how long you live, but what we do in the dash between the time we are born and the time we die. Not saying that we won't make mistakes along the way, but if we live long enough, what impact or legacy will you leave behind? In life, we are all given opportunities to show acts of kindness or selflessness. As Heather Yocum did when she did all that she could for Yolanda and her boyfriend, while others just stood around, made comments and watched. Another example was when I was taking care of business with Yolanda's car, I encountered two of the nicest people from Capital One Finance. A representative named Michelle sent me a card, stating that it was something she felt through the phone when speaking to me. She just wanted to send her condolences. I would later speak to another young lady named Jamie. She called when I was having a moment. I started not to answer, but I'm so glad that I did. I cried, shared things with her, and she shared things with me. We talked for about a half hour. Even when I told her that I'd better let her go before she lost her job, she just told me that I was fine and that it was a pleasure talking to me. She could have very easily got the information she needed from me and let me go. They will never know how much I appreciated them and the role they played in my healing. There are so many others, and God knows them one by one. I am forever grateful for them all.

I want people to understand the importance of organ donations. I am glad that Yolanda was able to help three people, Jim, Theresa and Jary. One recipient received a kidney and her liver, another her heart and lung, and another her other kidney. I want people to understand that it's not a bad thing. I've experienced it on both ends, my mom is still going strong after receiving a liver in 2011. I look at it as a partnership. The donor and the recipient needed one another to live on in some way. I'm glad to say that Yolanda brought awareness to people that had never considered it, but they have become registered donors.

Most importantly, I wanted people to see God. I stood on his promise and kept my mind on him and he did just what he said he would do. No, he didn't drop down out of the sky, but he ministered to me through song both before and after the accident. He spoke to my spirit through others. I could see him moving in situations that can't be explained. One example being after the passing of my friend and aunt, A week or so after my aunt passed my cousin, Edward Maxwell gave me a copy of a movie entitled A Question Of Faith. At the time I thought maybe it was to help me cope with their passing. But after thinking back on what the movie was about, I could see God moving way before the accident. You would have to see the movie to understand how I was strengthened through the message of the movie. This was just one of many instances that God made his presence known. Satan tried many times to take me to a dark place, but God always showed me the light at the end of the tunnel. If you trust him and open your heart to receive, he will give you a peace that passes all understanding. He'll help you find life beyond the tragedy.

If it be God's will and I'm blessed to see 2020, I will leave behind the pain, and embrace the life and legacy that continues on through me and many others. The fact that she won't be coming back will never change. But in the time that I have left, I can live a life with hopes of seeing her again and for that reason, I'm trading beauty for ashes.

Cassandra and Heather Yocum who was Yolanda's guardian angel at the accident.

Jary Jane is the recipient of Yolanda's heart and lung.

Theresa and Anthony McClary. Theresa is the recipient of one of Yolanda's kidneys.

Jim and Carol Powers – Jim is a recipient of Yolanda's kidney and liver.

Kim Whitlow, the coordinator from KODA and Cassandra

Mother's Day 2018 – Gifts of Flowers and a Medal from the Kentucky Organ Donor Affiliates Organization.

Her dad chauffeured Yolanda to her prom. A great day!

For more information about being an organ donor,

https://www.kyorgandonor.org/education-outreach/volunteer-network/

Here is the link to the registry: RegisterMe.org

Please let me know if I can assist you with other statistics or anything else you need!

The Race Of Life

The race is not given to the swift, but to the one that endures to the end. We are all running this race called life. And as any race you are in, it must end at some point. This particular race is a race of Faith and Perseverance. There are different types of races, short distances, middle distances and long distances. There are relay races, where other runners will pick up the baton and carry on until the end of their part of the race and then it continues on with the next runner that picks up the baton.

These races are taking place all over God's creation every day. If you are connected to the right power source when your race comes to its finish, there are no losers. Rather someone's race was a sprint or a marathon. The finish line is the same, Heaven. And there's only first place, Eternal Life.

No one knows how long their race will be, and there will be hurdles along the way. Jump over them, and if you should stumble and fall, get back up and keep running towards the mark of the high calling. Your Redeemer and loved ones will be at the finish line cheering you on. The race ain't over until God says that it's over. So, until then put your best foot forward, and run your best race. Stay connected to the creator, love and live a life that is pleasing to him. When the last race has been won, and we all get to heaven, what a day of rejoicing that will be.

Our last picture together, taken on Sunday, May 6, 2018. Yolanda, Danielle and Cassandra

www.ingramcontent.com/pod-product-compliance
Lightning Source LLC
Chambersburg PA
CBHW040015240426
43664CB00036B/4